Mélange Block

Denise Low

RED MOUNTAIN PRESS

The author is grateful to editors of publications where these
poems, sometimes in different forms, appeared previously:

Blue Lyra Review: "Crop Duster Plane"; *Coal City Review*:
"Advice"; *I-70 Review*: "Ghost Town"; *Kansas Time + Place*, ed.
Caryn Mirriam-Goldberg: "Report on the House at Cripple
Creek," Aug. 12, 2013; *I Was Indian: An Anthology of Native
Literature*, Volume II (Kanona, NY: Foothills Press, 2012): "After
the Genocide," "Walking with My Delaware Grandfather";
New Letters: "Recursive" ("At the Barre"); *Numéro Cinq*:
"Shooting Stars Wolf," "Sedimentation," "Cold," "West of Hays
City"; *The Sky Begins at Our Feet* (Ice Cube Press, 2011): "Lost."
Thorny Locust: "Flint Hills Lullaby"; *To the Stars Through
Difficulties: A Kansas Renga in 150 Voices* (Mammoth, 2012):
"Lost," "Touch"; *Virginia Quarterly Review*: "Parallax";
*The World Keeps Turning to Light: A Renga by the State Poets
Laureate of America* (Negative Capability Press, 2013):
"Minerals"("Starlight Captured in Stones"); *Yellow Medicine
Review*: "Another Custer Story: Cemetery," "Levitation" ("At
Dawn, the Deer"), "Winter Song."

ISBN 978-0-9799865-7-4
Printed in the United States of America
Second Printing

RED MOUNTAIN PRESS
Santa Fe, New Mexico
www.redmountainpress.us

The author is grateful to many family and friends who share love of poetry and literature, all of whom contribute to this work. Thank you to Susan Gardner and Devon Ross of Red Mountain Press for their heroic contributions to this and many other projects.

My husband Thomas Pecore Weso is present on every page.

TABLE OF CONTENTS

I

MINERALS

Starlight captured in stone awaits
mothers' dreams. When to ignite new flesh?

Women count winter bones
trapped in forests of fossil ferns,
choose some to breathe again.

Moon thaws distant snow.
Redbird shrieks alarm through white tides.
Lovers grapple under quilts.

Far away a ladle of wave breaks against quartz,
soft mirror of ancient dazzle.

River Leonid Showers overhill
UFOs flash Feather Lane
tribal cop's SUV is
on it.

Quartz-crystal sprinkle
dark pines hover glitter
woodland county lit-
up orb.

Phone camera off missed
Sasquatch on cable TV
his treetop moans
what next.

Riverview Circle dogs yowl
Saint Anthony burials
Little People trick nuns
Sun/Moon one.

Snake effigy mound upstream
here the clans Eagle Sturgeon
Crane Beaver Moose
Wolf Bear.

Tumbling Atlantis aliens
magnetize pyramids
stoned freaks stars
land here.

Particles vibrate inside limestone ledges
caroming at the speed of subatomic blinks.

I cannot hear the humming choir of solid mass
as I cannot hear your yesterday heart.

Fossil chalk crumbles across eons—
fern animals and mussel shells disassembling.

One day you caress my hand, cheek, breast.
You return recursively the next day and the next.

We exist in a visible spectrum of violet to red.
Limestone is buff. Precisely, it remembers tan.

When you leave, speed continues in atoms.
Spindles wobble and blur. I see gritty surface.

I test that heft. Density is the same as last year.
Heat of your skin sears. Motion stays in motion.

The rock wall holds its shape until gravity tugs
an imperceptible, off-balance weight.

⌘   ⌘   ⌘

Brother's walkingstick grinds grit ash
old film Journey to the Center of the Earth
rerun dream halfway along a twilight trek
as cones cross miles a dead museum of lava.
Prophecy of fire says he is halfway home.

Volcano penumbra detritus by starlight
geological cough generations ago captured
in place as home a concrete slab settles
over boulders galvanized roof over.
Upside downside all hard country still.

The hillside surprise: green springwater
alive with grass verbena elk-hoof moons
pecked Turtle outline black boulders
chiaroscuro glyph Shaman hands raised.
Power flows to dawn Suns each a god.

Molten core, radiant lines, magnetic field
reach catacombs of burning magma
calling red liquid ferrous mineral blood
Elk Turtle Holy Man and Brother beyond.
Strata sediments testify in his rock house.

⌘   ⌘   ⌘

Haze, volcanic aftermath, wreaths peaks, backlit
sunrise over craters. Daylight uncovers exteriors.
Night visions, interior suns, fade. Brother saved

from a frozen Hell. Hop this tuff stair to that

off-center black brick. And the next. The next.
Inside, Fourth World volcano slowly augurs up.

Matter / mater / Mother calibrated by star drizzle
Brother still walking unlit landscape cobbles
our distant relatives warmed wrenched open
broken monsters with hearts hidden in iron ore
until petroglyph Praying Man raising palms
against rock opens fingers catches and holds.

⌘   ⌘   ⌘

Lava springs will soon amaze Coronado
the field of chess-piece horsemen the pyres
funerary aftermath of a titan war lost.
Hills of Mars John Carter rescues Powell.

One magma leak across Arizona
vented seams three thousand interval years:
shield mountains lagoons double pyramids
Anasazis climb
                Bear rises into aurora sky.

Molten calendars pouring from the core
dried folded back caverns locked solid
spills left on set scenery forever-gone —
Brother returned, his hands in stars.

SEDIMENTATION: ALLIGATOR JUNIPERS

tree-skin sediments
oblong scales tiered
centuries old living shale

spiral rows mortared
circling pith of sap
guarding scant water

agate-ring years
seared drought forged
creased wrinkled torsos

PARALLAX

Eye of the backyard fox
trapped on night film
occipital orb flashes white
void encircled by night.

How geometry of round
fits cutout eclipse
exact sun-moon balance
equation of our planet.

Harvest moon's oval lens
casts hills in half light
rust scope to sight aim
how it shifts everything.

Volcanic Core

Throat of a volcano stands
frozen in a final bass note
sounds a muted threat
the old god's war song.

Boulders loiter around
like sheep lost in a meadow
of thin, shallow soil
fit only for silicate grasses.

Attached to mountainsides
pines tier distant planes
beyond this barren range.
Here is a place of spirits.

Elk pick among the ruins,
as mountain lions
nose their gamey scent.
Raven croaks. Then rain.

R IO L INDO: A GGREGATES

split schist   splay spiral   valley-reach calendar
my mother   mélange blocks   Redwood
Highway   river-mixed concrete   slate asphalt
not here Sunday

from her   pocket of mud   womb portal   silt
braided channels   broken shallows   railroad ties
gleaming tracks   intaglio on pasture   gradient
whines   pickups and semis   close distant
closer gone   traffic exhaust
tracers

Foss Creek spillway mowed crisp   down banks
thickets   ruddy blackberries   night raccoons
up branches ripe   confused profusion   flood
pooled   flesh nest burst   mulberries she hated
mauve stains   dissolve   eddy
spins away

nile lilies   upstream   stems bowing   what dead
sister   knowing   slender Isis   her women
servants   linen blue   scented vanilla   luminous
tongues   trumpet jasmine
mother sister close

gristle artichoke   gray-plume leaves   neon
bloom   olive tree's tongues   brittle tattle
garden ghosts count   crevice shade quiet
rattlesnakes outline   gopher scent   follow
invisible trail   death swallow   unfurling gravity
sister pulled   cenote   diamondback flicks
buried jade geodes

heron tilts sky   drinks mist   sky-blue   rights
itself   etched voice   scratch repeats   strato-
cumulus   indigo   overflow troughs   ponds
frogs pierced and gone   gray shadow water
wings   sulfur butterflies   soundless sister
mother scorch   hovering inner sight
what moon returns

Right Stepover Region   three slip-fault zones
lumber tumbling   one split board east   wall
sags   another shudders   rain mud stew
gravity sea   one tremor   one temblor   distant
shudder   swamps   string intervals   sister's
violin scales   shifting taut   catgut strings release
lilies quake   sediments gel
tossed topsoil

Limerick Lane   volcanic rubble road   fluvial
plain   no outlet   Los Amigos Road   cherry tree
loaded   Queen Anne yellow and rouge   diesel
convoys   upcoast downcoast lava flow   hard-
ash   spit from underground   sun again
Foppiano's   pink granite marbles   pebble dice
hear rupture hum   what washed   what blown
sparks   catacomb pumice   what diagonal
sunrise   slant trellis sequences   motion
snakeskin   twisted profiled flat   S cord end
roil back into   serpent hiss   mountain cones
coiled rock graves   fire ring   what extinguished
hearth
Quetzalcoatl gone

1926   Frank and Ernie's bar   Geyserville
sepia eyes cocked   a trapper a cowboy a cook a
miner   standing not smiling   looking past walls
past sister   past coastal ranges   past window
no daylight stasis past Mother's wedding
past wishes   North for ancestors
before I was born

beside the pump house   lily urns   each a mother
dust pollen   alchemy beside bricks   gladiolas
orange scatter   one day's draught   seconds
parceled   berries carried   each day   now
yesterday   somewhere existing   crows in olive
trees   ghosts   maybe sister mother
so much so far

Rioja:
Buried lava pulls
sun to its core.
Light and dark teeter.

Valpolicella:
Stair-step mountains shelter
innocent white blossoms,
the Garden of Eden.

Champagne:
Miniature explosions
from limestone cliffs
fizz this taffeta taste.

Medoza:
Canals carry clear water
through thin-air vineyards.
Mountain scents circle.

Barossa Valley:
Heat and river sediments
transmute time into
liquid brass current.

Hyde Vineyard:
Across the Carneros
fog spreads its cool touch.
Pomegranate clouds seep.

Rattlesnake Hill:
Pomo gamblers meet Juno.
Bloodlines mix rattler tracks.
Braided streams run diamonds.

Walla Walla:
In another desert arrives
a religion of isolation:
Age of Iron.

LOST

Lost? Yes, again the stars fall
on 13th Street where a house, now demolished,
was my home. I was young.

Funeral dirges sound from the building
and hearses ferry the dead. I was young
and swung on the backyard tire swing

one late October afternoon under red leaves
drifting like red stars to my feet.

I was young and then was gone like the house.
An old woman remains in my place.

COLD

A family burns chairs, clothes, and axes
but nothing stops the silent killer.
Neighbors find them frozen in bed.

Another year trees explode.
Crows fall from trees.
Lakota winter counts show a black-ink crow.
Ben Kindle writes, "*K'agi' o'ta c'uwi'tat'api.*"
Crows, they freeze to death.

This enemy seeps through sills and door jambs.
Chimney flues fill with its wrath.

North is its direction.
Nothing stops it from reaching
through flesh to the center of bone.

wickiup wickery
      silicate rough-crusted
driftwood enclosure
      bramble fencing repeating
burden basket inverted
sandbar charcoal
border brittle nest
night of braidings
legs twisted
where walks now
that meander
that autumn yellow child

    ⌘   ⌘   ⌘

flesh pentacle of arms, legs, head
pronged animal shape ambulant
live bones flesh-coated chalk

    ⌘   ⌘   ⌘

snow crystalline tumbling into
clotting sky's quick tumult
melted loss   disaster   cascades

    ⌘   ⌘   ⌘

asphodel spike of
black-tipped crane flock
asymmetrical tilt

flock bunched on salt marsh
plumage collected glistens
Easter light's tight beam center
kettling whorl
direction indirection listing
Pole Star sideways

⌘   ⌘   ⌘

neon yellow
king snake
cradled in
collapsed
rock edges

inside-out
crisp
rib-ridged
leaf
parchment
roll

What fails to coil
  spring of a childhood clock
  rattler dead under the car

What does not pivot
  pea-green cloud
    wisp-ends spindling

What does not recur
  oaks upended
  cars wadded

What unfolds
  dust whirlwind unturned
  roof tiles tiered square

What fades
  whistles blown through teeth
  hailstone salt on glass

INSIDE THE CRYSTAL

Crystal gazers seek   lovers
Coronado appears   gold dross
midnight mirage   Quivera lost
indigo flames   violet sun

Future past   cloud the orb
Cortez   arrives departs
Malintzin   lives dies
broken waves   powdered stars

Comancheria   burning blood
Santa Fe   obsidian red
volcanoes boil   hot cold
life death   the same ore

Rainbow portals spiral
sun moon   turning faces
betrayed lovers   reappear
laughter tears   glisten each night

⌘　　　　　　⌘　　　　　　⌘

Rufous humming buzz
serrated aspens jostle

overlapping confabulations

　　　headwaters.

⌘　　　　　　⌘　　　　　　⌘

Lodge pole pines
new growth
in forest ashes
lithe spokes
worth the journey
across plains.

⌘　　　　　　⌘　　　　　　⌘

Rain midafternoon
windowpane streaks.

Nuthatches down-spiral
bark layers
　　　listen for
　　　beetles.

⌘ ⌘ ⌘

Altar stones disappear.

Crows call in the canyon
so like magpies.

⌘ ⌘ ⌘

Reed greens flattened swathes
distant pines a quill-sewn border.

El Dora Stream
        Boulder Creek
gap between rock domes

wind roars a certain course.

⌘ ⌘ ⌘

Thunder's ripples reverberations
interruptions stumbles
before catastrophe.

Behind whipped cumulous
distant peaks sharpen
snowcap dazzles the loudest.

⌘   ⌘   ⌘

Gray-headed junco
rust-patched shoulders
unvoiced hops
        off-balance
        and up.

⌘   ⌘   ⌘

Watching sand banks crumble
left of center or right
or not at all

not predictable
        spill theories
        or not.

⌘   ⌘   ⌘

Each tree's dendritic leaves
laid over upended strata

covering unclocked beams
calibrations of oceans

inflections of verdance
as far as.

⌘ ⌘ ⌘

How water chooses streams
or sap funnels up
fire creases ethers
mountain chickadee-dee-ing
my hand divides its five
uneven directions, which
to follow.

Lord of wobble
     of entropy, decay
falling-down stairs

Lord of gait
     of canter
     of ladder steps
finish lines fumbles

of flesh
     sinew bound
sheathed and tenoned

of femurs
tapered angled

Lord of lungs
     deflated inflated
exhaled winded collapsed

Lord of fire
     of charred hearths
     cold ash clotted
melted boulders flung

Lord of lava geysers
Lord of all creation

By the river years ago, recursive in memory, a
finite moment, the past ended. Future began.

The river flowed south. You were a man's face
floating among stones.

By a river in autumn, willow leaves were yellow
whisks in updrafts. We were not alone.

Cottonwood boles twisted against banks, turtles
dozed in the roots, bark slivered into water.

The river sounded the swish of its name. You
waded the Neosho as it meandered east.

Two sandhill cranes fly overhead. Their legs
stretch straight behind as they swim through air.
Their grace is the river's.

No one saw flood-seined silt, gravel, broken
mussel pearls. I stayed, you left.

By the river I met you each day. I meet you each
day. I will be meeting you in invariant futures.

By the river leaves turn. Mud cracks pentagonal
shapes. You return and leave. The river remains.

By the river I was a child, I am grown. I
remember nothing, everything.

ANOTHER CUSTER STORY: CEMETERY

Past the pronged iron gate
a dark figure lifts his hat
flicks ashes on gravestones
inhales   says:

I am Etienne call me Stevens
          Nevin Custer's grandson
I am a hundred years old
I remember everything

His furrowed-map face turns
Blue eyes are buried embers
Jack oaks creak overhead
He exhales smoke   says:

We come from Ohio like you
Grandmother was Shawnee
from Opessa's Oldtown
Custer himself was Indian

He looks in my eyes   says:

Boston and Tom died that day
and Bloody Knife the Arikara
Their spirits live here
Never am I alone

Cheyenne cousins visit
In dreams they are brave
they are restless   I see them
in river currents   in lightning

He says:

Your family plots are next to mine
Blood remembers everything
You will forget nothing

He crushes his cigarette underfoot
unlatches the gate   walks North
Where he steps   red cedars
spring back into place

After Genocide

We find ourselves on a bare plain
neighbors shocked silent.

At last one man speaks.

> *The village was by the Mississippi.*
> *When the killing ended, two toddlers*
> *cried under a cookpot. The army recruit*
> *did not bayonet the girls but instead*
> *defied guns trained at his back.*
> *He took them and moved West.*

The soldier was his grandfather,
the younger baby was his mother.

⌘   ⌘   ⌘

Cold winter nights we sit in taverns
numbing our minds. We tell stories

about horses and whirlwinds. Or sit silent.
North wind drones war songs.

Anyone left by springtime is a friend
but sun streams from another god's heaven.

The children do not ask about grandparents.
We tell them nothing about Jackson's soldiers

or Paspahegh, Gnadenhutten, Yahoo Falls,
Horseshoe Bend, Washita, Wounded Knee

why they dream of turtles buried deep in mud.
We tell them to hush. Don't ask for much.

⌘   ⌘   ⌘

And so these few stories about my grandfather
remain:

*He ran in the schoolhouse door and out the back.
They had to call his mother to fetch him.*

He grew up on the ranch but his brother came first.

*He was too young for the Philippines, too old for the
Great War in Europe.*

*He worked in the railroad yards until hit hard by a
boxcar and injured.*

He disappeared weeks at a time and always returned.

He taught us to play poker and how to taunt:

Cut 'em thin, bound to win.

WALKING WITH MY DELAWARE GRANDFATHER

Walking home I feel a presence following
     and realize he is always there

that Native man with coal-black-hair who is
     my grandfather. In my first memories

he is present, mostly wordless,
     resident in the house where I was born.

My mother shows him the cleft in my chin
     identical to his. I am swaddled

and blinking in the kitchen light. So
     we are introduced. We never part.

Sometimes I forget he lodges in my house still
     the bone-house where my heart beats.

I carry his mother's framework
     a sturdy structure. I learn his birthright.

I hear his mother's teachings through
     what my mother said of her:

She kept a pot of stew on the stove
     all day for anyone to eat.

She never went to church but said
     you could be a good person anyway.

She fed hoboes during the '30s,
     her back porch a regular stop-over.

Every person has rights no matter
    what color. Be respectful.

This son of hers, my grandfather,
    still walks the streets with me.

Some twist of blood and heat still spark
    across the time bridge. Here, listen:

Air draws through these lungs made from his.
    His blood still pulses through this hand.

Today's brief rain is the flip side of sunny.
Clouds dampen the sweetgrass hill and depart.
Dust under the pine granulates even finer.
Red rings inside cedars record a thin year's spin.
Distant salt flats send scented emissaries.
The guide map legend script announces again
Entering the Great American Desert.

Within Earth
> Cold of Grandfather's hand,
> his mother's face, her voice,
> her hand cold on his face.

Within Sky
> Four directions of wind,
> sound of thunder set free,
> wind resounding with voices.

Within the North
> Cold pole star, fixed,
> snowy sawtooth peaks,
> spars of dazzling snow.

Within the South
> Neosho floodplain,
> seeds flooded in silt,
> river of lit green seeds.

Within the East
> After pitch-dark sunfall
> unformed void of night,
> dawn kindles ash.

Within the West
> Day's moment teetering,
> sun balances on hills,
> perfect whole circle.

Within Earth
> Touch of Grandfather's stone,
> thunder's voice, his hand,
> his mother's touch in my voice.

II

43

Flint Hills Lullaby

"Landscape has its own spirit; it is neither dead nor alive."

Thomas Weso

My grandparents continue to breathe here.
They exist in flood-harrowed grass.

Land is not dead, not living,
but something beyond calculation.

White strata collapse into ruins.
Thunderheads tumble dry counties.

Throngs of geese breathe one chorus.
Buried limestone transmutes into flint.

I am alone, caught in lay lines
of birthplace of continuum of loss.

Night brings dark-moon void.
May all our bones rest in peace.

Degas sits obliquely to the barre, rasping
charcoal against grained paper. Torsos
tangle in pastel flounces. Dancers
bend and bend as he doubles, triples lines.

He cannot sketch fast enough. All ways
the next luminous pose astonishes
his sideways glance. He grasps chalk —
not small waists, bosoms, oval faces.

No scarlet interrupts, no partners.
Only muted hues on the verge
of deepening. Another primrose girl rises,
lit by footlights. She spins out of reach.

Rue de Navarin: A View

River air carries tears of widows
from Caesar's Gallic Wars.
Monmartre's dome presses
against the pane, mountain-heavy.

In a far window a man waits.
Servants pantomime service —
a *casoulet* of lamb stew, napkins,
hands drawing tea from a samovar.

Another scent on air —
parchment going moldy
or is it sisal fittings for a galleon
filtering through these stone walls?

TOUCH

If I could touch the Milky Way
my hands could learn how sparks ignite.
I would learn syllables of dark.

If I could touch the sound of crickets
history of autumn would resound.

If I could touch November moonlight
I could prophesize the winter's course.
I would stack woodpiles under the eaves.

If I could touch my distant lover
our breath would turn to river's mist.

HACKBERRY EMPERORS OUTBREAK

> "Hackberry Emperor butterflies need to consume salt
> to complete their sexual development." Chip Taylor

Speckled beige lords ingest bark,
feast of salt hackberry crumbs.

Regal flutterers sport sparrow livery,
sepia riffling hot breezes.

In amaranth-edged bracken
ripple scores of ornate wingbeats,

minked tints, *punto in aria* lace,
scalloped silk. Dancers minuet.

Seed-black eyes open, they clasp each other,
clutch and join. Fall headlong into sky.

WINTER PLAINS SONG

Milky Way gyre spins stars
around black absence of motion:

My sister's soul may appear
in that invisible, pulsing core.

Fox tracks in snow lead North,
a dark timeline against white expanse

then vanished. Winter lessons arise
from simple elements. Matter freezes.

Deep space is absolute cold.
Nothing exists without memory.

Buffalo Calf Woman can dazzle
the horizon-edge of known reality.

Ice tides lap a gray sea sky.
Light descends down, inward, out.

Ghosts float above ground.
Deer waver in sunrise fog over asphalt.
Front-on, only ears show,
sideways, slanting northward.
Full bodies appear—soft-tan fur,
solid torsos, brown cherub eyes.
They move obliquely in pale light.

They could fall to curbs but veer
to cedars. Hooves never touch.
I plod behind them, earthen,
lost in gravity and night glum.
Sun glimmers, glitter mist fills air,
they rise.

Apache men pass us on the trail,
move easily among boulders.
So begins a season of prayer
Christmas noon in the desert.

We linger on the mountain's flank,
in gardens of creosote and saguaro.
We witness weathered petroglyphs,
bighorn sheep, white crosses for stars.

Blood-red stones are petrified hymns,
slow roilings of earth, *sotto voce*.
Cactus wrens converse from cholla.
We hear tunes of our own raspy breath.

Evening, our procession reverses.
The four men pass us, homeward,
nodding at us northern visitors
before darkness laps away light.

Heart of Water

A few drunks splash down,
night fishermen
never to be seen again.

A spiral turns underwater
opens a circle
of downward ripples.

Once I touched
the quicksand portal
cold tentacles reaching

through glacial currents —
ancient water filled with
spirits and their grief.

I pulled my hand away.
Years later I still feel
fingertips burn.

EMBER

for William Oandasan (1947-1992)

Fugitive poem on the table
perforated, detached, untitled —

"long ago black bears /
 sang around our lodge fires" —

this half-life we share,
sketched Round Valley map —

 "tonight they dance /
alive through our dreams" —

roils of Neosho current
blue roans against hills

what you set loose in my ears
what you left in paper sheaves.

Your words flame in my hands.
They circle the fire's heart ,

what you knew.
What you dove into.

HUES

I look into my lover's eyes.
Like lit sumac, they catch fire.
Our glances kindle scarlet.

My tongue tastes sea-blue.
My hands dip in purple water.
Elderberry blooms next to us.

Alfalfa flowers spread lemon.
Mountain winds smell of snow
while before us lie miles of sage.

Our legs entwine into bramble.
When we kiss, fragrance becomes
the skin's sun-heat smell.

A cinder pyre burns away the west
until again we are blind.

SOLO CATBIRD

voice mirror
polished tin
burrs tattles

exact coins
sound barter
no change

high wire
acrobat
pivots dips

trills odes
scratches sobs
quicksilver

lightning
mercury flash
exit

REPORT ON THE HOUSE AT CRIPPLE CREEK

The mined-out mountain shifts against gravity.
Blasted rock terraces sprout scrubby grass.

A large raven sidles by, tail feathers down.
We are sorry to make it nervous.

Hummingbirds dive at my orange blouse, veer
away, buzzing pizzicato.

Amaranth is seeded. Geraniums sprinkle stars .
At night their flames rise in constellations.

Foxes burrow in granite catacombs under us.
At night soft weight shifts on the porch.

A spider lives in the sink.
Husks of brown moths litter the porcelain.

Out the window, hundreds of peaks intersect—
asteroids, mica sheets, bolts of blue silk.

GHOST TOWN

At ten-thousand feet, barroom stories unfold
the repeating tale—gin, hunting knife, blood.

Foxes look to see if people are ghosts or alive.
Storefront lights blink through the night.

Fork-tailed swifts flicker into existence,
quick optics visible in sun-shafts, then not.

Descendants sell trappings of the dead —
bottles, pick-axes, rusted bolts, clocks.

The museum raises funds to save the brothel,
its red-velvet histories. Priests are gone.

On the hillside, tombstones whiten under snow,
lodes of granite sinking into final cold oblivion.

The challenge is to rewrite the Bible, think big,
      fill unrelenting spaces with murals.
        Swathes of sun-yellow stubble glow,
pale hue illuminated into brilliance.

I grew up in gessoed landscape without peaks,
      people lost in swells of dried seas,
        wandering stories of seven-year droughts,
dust devils, escape, baptism by prairie fires.

Patches of pine windbreaks slide into gullies
      where white houses huddle among barns.
        Bright corn circles drain Ice Age water.
Weathered outbuildings shelter crazy prophets.

Wending bluestem and datura outlast summer.
      One drought, buffalo grass fills in blanks.
        All else turns to trail ruts and shibboleths
Quartelejo Pueblo, Fort Zarah, Fort Wallace.

loops its nervous buzz
one green-shag row, the next,
tracing perfect graphs,

puffing powdered sugar
through heavenly blue air.
Poison settles on corn.

Inside the cab, radio thumps
bass and combustion.
The fuel gauge counts time.

Beyond the irrigated swatch
sandstone dunes, shrubbery,
hawks on cottonwoods.

This is how each day passes —
measured, remote,
solo, slow.

ICARUS IN PARADISE

Once I watched a man on back roads
sputter aloft in a glider, a balsawood
contraption with a lawnmower motor.

He lived in isolation with take-off hills
around him too much to resist. He was Icarus
doomed to short flights, companion to squabs,

far lower than hawks. Rising, he felt sparks
from western winds singe his teeth.
Sun burned his cheeks. High over the pond

he saw reflections of his papery wings—
white caplets leaping on murky green.
Geese squawked from his shadow.

Past a flinty cuesta he finally heard it.
His clatter settled into a steady hum.

MISSED: AUTOBIOGRAPHIES

motorcycle sideways skid
     jugular not severed

cursive maiden name
     not engraved verso

Grandmother's amethyst ring
     violet eyes not ash

wall clouds on water
wisp not spindling

hedge of elder
buds unripened

pink-tucked ivory bodice
     unbuttoned lace

brandied peaches frozen
champagne flutes empty

silver frame unshiny
     picture window white

SAINT PATRICK'S AGAIN

Live jazz at El Fresco is one guy, electric plinks,
until he turns off the switch, closes his eyes,

and warbles a boy's tenor, wood-flute tones,
pure séance hymns from before Christians.

Rowdies at the bar stop fighting and stare
as seawater washes through the room,

seeping through floorboards to serpent dens.
The chorus stirs spirits from family lore.

Desmond, Big Miller, James MackGehee—
all rise from steerage and sing with the lords.

Next performance is a poet reciting,
"The Luck of the Irish," blue eyes snapping:

"Once I journeyed to the Cliffs of Moher."
I follow him to a rocky precipice, pause,

then jump to dizzy foam tides below, fall,
keep falling into this slow, heartbreaking solo.

ADVICE

Knot thread
one loop
loop again
roll between your fingers
with spittle.

Flatten the end
between your teeth.

Hold the needle's slippery silver
steady.

Aim
for the eye.

Only after my mother died did faded
photographs reveal her past:

her Delaware father with coal-black hair
her mother a coquettish girl
her Irish-German grandfather in an elegant suit
and a portrait, a blotted out figure beside her—
the boy who did not become my father.

I return grandparents and unknown cousins
to their perpetual rest in folios.

Tomorrow I will see coreopsis drizzle yellow
mist into distance but not see what sights lie
beyond.

PEYOTE

Bitter hope
laces tea.
Peyote dust
thins blood
tilts sky.

Star-streams
touch ground.
Cedar crackles.
Spiral cinders
sizzle alive.

People below
seem small
water bird
water drum
far away.

Frantic
heartbeats
quick breath
blood sings
my own voice.

Help me.
Heal me
oh Lord
please
heal
us
all.

Mélange Block is set in Palatino,
a 20th century font designed by Hermann Zapf
based on the humanist typefaces of the Italian
Renaissance and named for the 16th century
Italian master of calligraphy Giambattista Palatino.

"Reproductive Invariance" is based on paintings and writings of Per Kirkeby, the exhibit at the Phillips Collection (2012) and his book *Writings on Art* (Spring Publications, 2012): 1, 82.

"Minerals" begins with a quotation from a renga by Alan Birkelbach, in *To the Stars: A Kansas Renga in 150 Voices,* edited by Caryn Mirriam-Goldberg (Mammoth, 2012).

"Branching" uses a short quotation from Francis Ponge's *Le Pré.*

"Lost Gods" is informed by descriptions by David Low of Anthill Farms Winery, Healdsburg, California.

"Cold" refers to a Winter Count by Ben Kindle, Oglala, who learned the Winter Count from his grandfather Afraid-of-Soldier, quoted in Martha Warren Beckwith, "Mythology of the Oglala Sioux," *Journal of American Folklore* 43 (1930). The year is 1789.

"St. Patrick's" references a reading by Michael Heffernan in Fayetteville, March 17, 2013. The quotation is from "The Luck of the Irish," *Walking Distance* (Lost Horse Press, 2013). Used with permission.

"Hackberry Emperors" begins with a quotation from Chip Taylor, naturalist, "A Bumper Crop of Butterflies," 25 May 2013, *Lawrence Journal World.*

"Recursive" is based on the exhibit Degas's Dancers at the Barre: Point and Counterpoint, The Phillips Collection, Washington D.C., October 1, 2011–January 8, 2012.